SURVIVAL 101

The Simple Guide to Saving Your Own Life When Disaster Strikes

by Marcus Duke

Galleon Publishing
Atlanta, GA

www.galleonpublishing.com

With love and many thanks for my wife, Katie,
and all of our students

TABLE OF CONTENTS

SECTION SUMMARIES

SECTION I. PREPARE FOR THE EXPECTED

In this chapter, we'll discuss what is involved in building a basic emergency stockpile of food and supplies. Also: should you head for the city or the countryside?

SECTION II. CREATING FIRE

Here we address several potential methods of creating a fire. It's not all about rubbing two sticks together.

SECTION III. DEHYDRATION AND YOU

More important than food or shelter, you will die after a few days without water. This chapter talks about ways to get the most out of limited water resources. Also: what to do when you're lost at sea?

SECTION IV. SECURING SHELTER

Outside of food and water, having some level of protection and safety from nature's elements is an absolute essential.

SECTION V. MAKESHIFT MEDICAL CARE

When you're in a disaster situation, it's often impossible to access proper medical care. This section addresses a few simple things you should try to have on hand.

SECTION VI. HANDLING A COMMON NATURAL DISASTER

How you react to a disaster will depend greatly on the type of event, but this chapter gives you some good basic rules for dealing with the most common types of natural disasters. Securing your home, insurance issues, etc.

SECTION VII. THE REVIEW

Here we go over some of the key points from the previous five chapters and I will suggest some additional resources for you to explore.

SECTION I.
Prepare for The Expected

Survival experts, when asked, will tell you they do not prepare for an "unexpected" crisis, they prepare for the "expected" crisis.

In other words, it is not a matter of if... but a matter of when.

You may have heard of people called preppers or doomsday preppers, many of whom have a very specific scenario in mind and only seek to prepare themselves for that type of event. Some are convinced it will be a major earthquake, some worry about a flood or perhaps a super-disease. Others focus more on a collapse of civil society, certain that the world's economy is on the very brink of ruin.

The truth is that trying to guess the type of disaster that will strike is much less important than having good general survival knowledge and doing the very basic preparation work needed to keep yourself and your family safe and protected. That way, if the stock market crashes or if you find yourself staring down the eye of a category 5 hurricane, you'll know what to do and will have the tools to make it through in one piece.

The purpose of this text is to give you that very basic knowledge that you will need to keep yourself and your family alive.

Human society is not all that different from an ant hill. When it gets disrupted, it will slowly put itself back together. The ants will scatter, and then they will return and rebuild.

A crisis will bring out the worst, and the best, in any group of people. A true collapse of society will be followed by a brief period of anarchy, with looting, gangs looking to profit and mindless followers that are looking for someone to lead and take care of them. You must seek to avoid all of this by being self-sufficient and well supplied with materials that not only get you through the early stages of chaos, but that can sustain you for extended periods of time.

Supplies run out eventually and you must realize that whatever calculations you have made will not be totally accurate. You could run out of food or batteries faster than you have estimated for any number of reasons. Stress causes people to eat more, and you can expect to require more calories than normal because of increased physical labor you'll likely find yourself engaged in. Friends, neighbors and even strangers will drain your supplies if they know you have anything to spare. Which leads us to a question I'll address shortly: Is it a good idea to help others and let them know you have supplies?

Is Stockpiling Smart?

In short, the answer is yes. Obviously, when a crisis hits you must have enough materials to sustain life for a period immediately following the initial event, and then have the materials, supplies and equipment to maintain life for extended periods beyond that.

Your objective is to provide shelter, water, fire, food, protection and medical care for your family and yourself. Having a reasonable stockpile of select, high-value materials can be the difference between life and death. A full list of items you should consider when building a stockpile can be found later in this text.

You must also stockpile items to barter with; depending on the type of disaster, money may become worthless. Therefore, when stockpiling you should consider items that you may not have a need for, but that others might. Consider things like tobacco products, drinkable alcohol, ammunition/weapons and certain prescription drugs or medical supplies.

Remember that once the city, state or even country's infrastructure is crippled, you will have no electricity, water from your city's treatment plant, gas, Internet, cell phones, limited fuel for vehicles and no emergency services. Really think about what that will mean.

Where Should You Keep Your Stockpile?

There are advantages and disadvantages of keeping your stockpile inside your home.

One disadvantage is that you may find yourself dipping into the supplies for everyday use, a practice that can leave you underprepared when disaster strikes. Plus, depending on your living situation, you may not have proper space to store all the supplies you'll need.

Keeping everything at home could also make you into a target if others know you have a sizable stockpile. On the flip side, when supplies are in your home that means they are under your control and readily available to be utilized in a disaster situation.

Regardless of where you keep your stockpile, it is recommended that you do not advertise the fact you are well fortified with supplies and materials. You do not want to be the person everyone turns to for help when times get tough.

Having alternative storage areas makes sense if you control the location. However, be sure to thoroughly think through how you will access the materials you've stashed away. If, for example, you use a commercial storage facility and a disaster strikes you may have no control over access to the facility. Storage facilities are also prime targets for looters and other criminal elements during a crisis.

Any viable offsite storage areas must be under your control, such as underground bunkers near or on your property or on property that you can reasonably expect to have unlimited access to.

You must also learn how to plot locations on a map using a compass, because you cannot expect to rely on GPS devices. Satellites and cell services will be some of the first to fail in certain disaster situations.

Which is Better: Rural or Urban?

Both environments have their advantages and disadvantages, and in some cases, it may depend on where a person feels most comfortable. Rural settings obviously have more privacy, and fewer people to deal with.

In an urban environment you will have crowds of people that may be trying to evacuate the city. Stockpiling can be less problematic in the country because you can cache supplies in the ground, on your own property or neighboring land where you would have access.

Urban dwellers can, however, more easily look for and obtain supplies, tools and other materials in abandoned apartments and other buildings. People may abandon homes and businesses in hopes of finding a safer location or have simply evacuated the city out of panic, leaving useful materials behind. In terms of long-duration survivability, apartment dwellers can have limited sized gardens on their balconies, and can forage for food supplies throughout the city.

Most people would likely pick a rural setting if they have that option. In fact, many hardcore preppers relocate to larger parcels of land to accommodate their survival bunkers, and to get away from others so they can train with weapons and practice their drills in seclusion.

From a completely logistical standpoint, a rural setting makes more sense, particularly in the long term disaster scenario. You'll have more land to cultivate gardens and raise livestock, and you'll have more water sources and less interaction with other people.

Those living in a city may be forced to find another place to live or have to evacuate the city altogether because of looting, other crimes and possibly fires and structural damage to buildings whereas, if you live in the country there is no need to leave and likely nowhere to go anyway.

Additionally, the right rural area could be designed to more easily secure your supplies against intruders.

The following is a list of items that keep immediate needs in mind as well as sustaining life after your supplies have been depleted. Where the item is on the list is not an indication of its importance.

Essentials for Survival Immediately Following a Disaster

- If possible, try to store at least a 30-day supply of food to give yourself time to appraise the situation and make long terms plans. Use dehydrated foods as much as possible because they do not consume as much space or weight as canned foods and they have an extended shelf life. Keep in mind however; dehydrated foods will require water for their preparation, in most cases.
- Water is essential and you must have at least a gallon a day per person, you must also have the means to collect, filter and purify various water sources and if possible begin construction on your own water well that you control.

- Two to four gallons of household chlorine bleach with 5% chlorine as an active ingredient for water purification; you must also have a medicine dropper to measure the bleach.
- Heavy tarps for emergency shelter, and repairs to your structure
- Clothes and accessories for all seasons
- Charcoal grills and or camp stoves with plenty of fuel
- Garbage bags (specifically: ultra-durable contractor bags)
- Coffee filters for water (particulate) filtration
- Several vials of 2% percent liquid iodine for emergency water purification
- Stainless steel canteens (one per person)
- Emergency heat blankets (one per person)
- Various means to start fires and do not rely solely on matches you should have a magnesium stick and other alternative means with which to start fires.
- Weapons for personal protection
- Personal hygiene supplies such as bars of soap, toothpaste, wet wipes for body washing when water is in short supply including hand sanitizer
- Candles and lanterns for illumination (include adequate fuel for the lanterns)

- Several first aid kits (include a quality topical antiseptic such as Betadine, also include a suture kit for sewing up wounds)
- Insect repellent and netting

Materials and Equipment for Sustainability

- Bags of lime for odor control in garbage pits and latrines
- Heirloom seeds so you can begin growing your own food (ensure the seeds are heirloom and not from hybrid plants)
- Some basic tools to use in gardening
- Knives to butcher wild game or farm raised animals
- Fishing supplies (a simple kit with a small pole can be purchased for under $15 at most big box stores)
- Picks and shovels for burying garbage and digging latrines
- A wood saw
- Sizable amount of activated charcoal (for water filtration) which is available at any pet or retail store that sells aquariums. Activated charcoal is used in aquarium filtration systems.
- Heavy rope, twine and string in various amounts

- Various cooking utensils and assorted pots and pans
- Heavy work gloves

The lists above are, of course, not universal and must be adapted for your personal situation and location. Once again, remember your supplies will run out, whether you have stockpiled a year's worth or for only a month. The more you have of something the more you tend to use and fail to ration because you feel you have an unlimited supply. You will tend to give to others because of your large stockpile. Be aware of this, ration from the beginning, and always keep your family's survival at the forefront.

You should always keep life sustaining essentials in the front of your mind when gathering supplies: shelter, water, food, medicine, and fire.

If you are facing an extended-duration crisis or total societal collapse, expect your situation to evolve significantly over time. It will be up to you to decide at what point your focus will shift from mere survival to the sustainability of long-term living.

You will, no doubt, have to begin foraging from surrounding areas to supplement your supplies. It's reasonable to expect that many people will flee in panic and some will have left valuable materials and supplies behind. Look for gardens and farm animals wandering loose that can be used as a food source. You will have to decide at some point when to begin creating your own food source, which is why it is important to gather seeds and locate possible sources of farm animals early on so that you can be among the first to commandeer them and begin raising animals in the aftermath.

SECTION II.
Creating Fire

Fire is extraordinarily important for human survival. It provides heat, light, the ability to cook meat and to purify water. Fires can signal rescuers and scare off dangerous wild animals.

Keeping a supply of matches and other fire-starting tools on hand is important. However, we're not always going to be in the most ideal of circumstances, surrounded by all of our survival assets, when a real disaster strikes. Therefore, it is important that you know how to start a fire using a variety of resources.

There are many ways to start a fire beyond simple friction. If you are proficient at rubbing two sticks together to create a blaze, then I say go for it. However, keep in mind that it's trickier than it looks in the movies.

For my money, there are several more surefire (pardon the pun) ways to get a campfire started. I always try these before I ever start rubbing twigs together.

You can start a fire using car batteries and batteries from handheld electronic devices, all you need is a spark and a highly combustible material, such as magnesium shavings, hand sanitizer that contains alcohol, alcohol wipes or petroleum jelly.

Fires can also be started by focusing sunlight to greater intensity, using a magnifying glass, pieces of glass, headlight fixtures, eyeglasses and even water. This method, however, requires a lot of cooperation from Mother Nature and should be tried in only the most ideal circumstances with direct mid-day sunlight.

Before you start working on the spark, make sure you have assembled a viable tinder nest out of any available materials that catch fire easily: dry grass, leaves, bark shavings, bits of paper. This is where you want to direct your generated spark, and you'll need enough material for the fire to begin to take root while you slowly add additional fuel.

Generally, I will gather a full two handfuls of materials before trying to start a fire, but I'll only use about one-half of a handful for the initial spark. I will keep the rest of the material very close by and use it to rapidly nurse the fragile ember into a full-grown flame.

Once your spark becomes an ember, oxygen and additional combustible fuel are the ingredients to build a real fire. Be cautious not to crush your ember with fuel and deprive it of oxygen. Blow and fan the ember as needed to encourage growth.

Friction and Fuel

One of the absolute simplest ways to get a fire started in through the use of impact friction.

Put some hand sanitizer or squeeze an alcohol wipe (found in most first aid kits) on any combustible material and generate a spark by striking metal-on-metal or stone-on-metal. You must, of course, direct the spark toward the combustible material.

Alcohol burns quickly and the flame is difficult to see in sunlight. To increase the burn time rub some lip balm such as Chapstick or petroleum jelly on the material. Petroleum jelly on a cotton ball can burn for up to four minutes, thus giving you ample time to add more combustibles to the flame.

Starting a Fire with a Battery

First off, using car batteries to start fires should be a last resort, only pursued when the need for a fire outweighs the inherent dangers of messing around with a car battery. Unlike magnetos, car batteries and other batteries, store direct current to be used on demand. Car batteries generate an explosive gas and can combust when exposed to spark or flame, so use caution and take reasonable protective measures such as protective eyewear, gloves or use some type of shield to separate the battery from any sparks, heat or flame.

You begin by connecting a conductive material between the negative (black) and positive (red) posts on a car battery. Do not allow the wire ends to touch until you are ready to start the fire. You should never attempt to start the fire near the battery; you must have enough wire to connect to both posts allowing plenty of space between the fire and battery. You can use jumper cables to create a spark by tapping the ends together once connected to the car battery posts. The cables must be long enough to reach a tinder pile on the ground. The sparks can ignite tinder or you can briefly hold the cable ends together to generate enough heat to ignite the tinder.

When dealing with a less powerful battery, such as one found in a cellphone or portable electronic device, steel wool is an ideal material that can be used to create a fire. The steel wool itself will burn while conductive wire simply generates heat or sparks to start tinder.

The steel wool or wiring must touch both posts on any battery to create a connection and once the wire ends are connected to each other they must be quickly put in contact with the dry tinder or combustible material.

Above all, be careful when using a battery to start a fire. It is a fast and easy, but also a potentially dangerous method.

Starting a Fire with Sunlight

For this method, the most ideal solution will required you to obtain the glass from an auto headlight and the reflective bulb casing. Remember, this method only works with adequate sunlight and patience.

The glass along with the reflective case is used to amplify the sun's ray to ignite dry tinder. If the glass is mostly intact, leave it in place and carefully place dry tinder where the bulb would normally be located. If the glass from the light is completely broken away, position shards so sunlight flows through the pieces onto the reflective case. The glass in combination with the highly reflective material will amplify sunlight, which in turn will ignite the tinder.

If you don't have a headlight, pieces of glass, bags of water/ urine, or a magnifying glass can be used to focus the sun's rays on your dry tinder. Once you see smoke, you will soon see an ember. Gently blow on the ember to create a flame. Add pieces slowly to increase the fire's size.

Use a Bicycle

Many ordinary bikes will have a device that powers a headlight as the wheels spin, this is typically called a magneto. It works by generating a direct current with a series of magnets imbedded inside a metal casing. The magneto provides current only when the wheel is spinning.

The magneto has a small device that spins when in contact with the side of the rotating bike wheel; this causes the small turbine inside the magneto to spin, thus generating current. That current then flows through some light gauge wiring to the headlight bulb.

First, cut the wire as close to the headlight as possible so that you have enough length to reach your pile of tinder. The current generated by the magneto, instead of illuminating the bulb, will transmit heat to ignite the tinder. You must make a connection with the wire ends while they rest in the tinder pile. You can enhance the fire starting method by squeezing an alcohol wipe over the tinder just before you begin spinning the wheel to create current. Alcohol evaporates quickly so this must be the last step before spinning the wheel.

When you're ready, turn the bike upside down so you can spin the wheels by hand using the pedals. You may have to change gears to build the greatest momentum.

SECTION III.
Dealing with Dehydration

Note: This information is not to be considered medical advice, and the amounts noted are only approximations. Consult with your medical professional for more detailed information and advice.

Simply, dehydration occurs when a body loses more fluids than it takes in. Excessive and rapid loss of bodily fluids can be caused by extreme sweating brought on by exertion in hot weather and from illnesses, which cause vomiting, diarrhea, and fever.

Dehydration in its early stages can be reversed by consuming water. Headaches, flushed skin and blurred vision are typical symptoms of mild to moderate dehydration. Severe to extreme dehydration does require medical attention. Untreated severe dehydration results in systematic organ failure, which leads to death. You can begin experiencing signs of mild dehydration after just a few hours if you are sweating heavily and are not replacing lost fluids quickly enough.

During an average day, individuals receive a portion of their daily fluid intake through coffee, juices, flavored drinks and certain foods. According to the Mayo Clinic an average male, living in a relatively temperate zone requires about 13 cups of liquids, (not necessarily all water) while the average female requires roughly nine cups of liquids daily. Thirteen cups is a little over 2.5 quarts or roughly three liters while nine cups is a little over two quarts or roughly 2.2 liters. The recommended daily intake varies based on body size, medical conditions and exertion level.

Survival experts will recommend that a relatively healthy adult will need at least 2 quarts of water daily, just for hydration, if water is your only source of liquid while in a survival situation. This amount takes into account eating and physical activity that is required for self-rescue and performing numerous other survival related tasks. When planning any outdoor adventure plan on one gallon of water daily for each individual. The one-gallon standard takes into account daily hygiene needs such as sponge baths and brushing of teeth. Your daily water needs can vary based on climate, activity level and any underlying medical conditions.

Surviving With a Limited Water Supply

Once you realize your situation is dire, water rationing must be begin at once. Do not consume any foods until you have established a reliable water source. Food, and in particular high protein foods such as energy bars, requires fluids to aid in digestion.

Stay in the shade and limit activities during the hottest part of the day. You want to avoid excessive sweating, which of course removes precious fluid from your body. The body sweats to cool itself by the evaporation of sweat on the skin. That evaporation is accelerated when your skin is exposed to sun and wind.

The more quickly sweat evaporates, the faster the body produces more. You must slow down sweating and evaporation to conserve your body's fluids. There have been documented cases where people have survived in access of three days, with no water at all, by finding protection from the sun and wind and by limiting movement.

You can easily become dehydrated in cold temperatures as well. Your breath vaporizers in cold weather, which illustrates how the body loses moisture from exhaling, and over exertion will cause you to exhale more moisture. In cold climates dress so you can regulate your body temperature by removing or adding layers. You do not want to sweat heavily under your clothes in cold weather.

How Long Can You Survive Without Water?

The actual time a person can live on little to no water depends on how well they conserve bodily fluids. As I've already stated, certain climate conditions will accelerate fluid loss. So, naturally, a person could conceivably survive a bit longer in a more humid less windy/sunny environment.

Most experts concur that the length of time before severe dehydration sets in is three days (72 hours). At that point, without medical treatment, the condition is likely fatal.

That time frame assumes certain facts: that the person is of average size and health, etc.

In some cases, you may be able to slow down the onset of severe dehydration for up to another day or two if you remain well shaded and you avoid virtually all physical activity.

The bottom line is that survival depends on how well your body can conserve fluids, but no matter what you only have a couple of days before you're in extremely serious trouble.

What about Seawater?

Rainfall, rivers, lakes, streams, green edible vegetation and even seawater are all sources of potential hydration if you find yourself in a survival situation. We addressed fresh water purification through the use of household bleach or iodine in an earlier section. Seawater cannot, however, be consumed unless you have desalinated the water first.

Seawater or saltwater contains up to three times the amount of sodium that the human body contains. If you consume saltwater as a means to survive, you will have made a fatal mistake.

Once your body takes in saltwater it will begin flushing all fluids from cells in an attempt rid the body of the massive amounts of sodium. Urination is how the body tries to rid itself of large amounts of sodium. Your cells will soon be depleted of all fluids, and your kidneys will not be able to handle the task. Once the cells and organs have lost 15 percent or more of their fluids, they begin to fail. Trying to avoid urination will NOT prevent your body from flushing fluids from its cells.

So let me repeat this: do not drink untreated seawater, you will die!

However, there are two primary ways seawater can be made safe to drink while in an extreme survival situation. One involves boiling seawater and collecting the steam, which is purified/distilled water. The other method is using a solar distiller. Both methods rely on evaporation. Only pure water evaporates, leaving sodium and other contaminates in the seawater.

To desalinate seawater by boiling you will need a pot to boil water in, fire to boil water with, a small collection container such as a glass, a piece of clear plastic sheeting and two small weights.

1. Place the collection cup with a weight in the bottom in the center of the pot.

2. Carefully pour seawater around the cup being careful not to get any in the cup. The weight in the cup keeps it from floating once water is poured around it. Fill the pot halfway so boiling water does not splash into the cup.

3. Place the plastic over the top of the pot of water and seal as tight as you can with string, rubber band or heavy-duty tape; you want a tight seal to keep the steam contained.

4. Take the second weight and place on the plastic over the collection glass in the pot. You want to form a slight depression in the plastic.

5. Then place a hole in the plastic over the cup. Begin heating the water. As the water heats, steam will condensate on the topside of the plastic and make its way toward the depression in the plastic and through the hole into the collection cup. Once most of the seawater has evaporated, let cool and remove the collection cup. You can repeat as often as needed.

Variations of this method include hanging plastic close to or over the boiling pot so the steam collects on the plastic. Once it condensates on the plastic, you can absorb it with cloths or allow it to drip from the plastic sheeting into a container.

An alternative method involves placing a clean cotton cloth over a boiling pot of saltwater to collect the steam. Squeeze the cloth into a container or directly into your mouth.

The way you conduct your boiling purification will depend on what resources you have available to you. Just make sure that you drink the steam you're producing, not the saltwater.

A more crude method, in case you do not have access to a fire, is to evaporate seawater in a container and collect the condensation. This method requires a collection cup, large glass bowl (any bowl or pot will work, though not as effectively), two small weights, string/tape/large rubber band, sheet of clear plastic and sunlight.

1. Take the collection cup and place a weight in it and place in the center of the bowl. Pour seawater around the glass and fill the bowl two thirds full, being careful not to get any in the glass.

2. Place the clear plastic over the bowl and seal tight by wrapping tape/ string/rubber band around the edge to seal it to the bowl. Next, take the second weight and place over the collection cup, to create a depression in the plastic. Then put a hole in the plastic directly over the collection cup.

3. Place the bowl in direct sunlight. It will take several hours for evaporation to start. Moisture will collect on the plastic and begin dripping into the cup. This water is purified because only pure water evaporates.

SECTION IV.
Securing Shelter

The rule of three for survival dictates that you cannot survive longer than three minutes without air, three hours without shelter, three days without water and three weeks without food. The times are based on averages of course and can vary significantly depending upon circumstances.

While it is quite conceivable that you could survive in a temperate climate for longer than three hours without shelter, the very term "shelter" is subjective and something as simple as getting out of the hot sun by getting under a tree is considered shelter. Hell, the clothes you are wearing can be considered shelter.

To put it in the most basic terms, you cannot survive for very long if you do not find some type of cover from the hot sun, cold rain, wind or frigid temperatures. The elements are your enemy.

Ideally, you will have supplies, materials and tools with you to help you build and maintain a shelter.

However, you might also be in a situation in which some type of natural shelter is readily available.

For purposes of having a discussion about securing basic survival shelter, let's say that you've gotten hopelessly lost in the woods during a hike and have no expectation of immediate rescue.

You will need some protection from animals, insects and the weather if you have to spend the night in the forest alone. Let's also assume that you've left your snuggly sleeping bag and nifty professional camping tent back in your vehicle.

The first order of business is to select a suitable location and setup a campfire. As we've already discussed, creating fire isn't easy but there are many ways to get the spark you'll need.

Once you have a burning fire to provide heat and ward off animal intruders, begin work on constructing a crude frame out of whatever materials you have available. If needed, you can construct this very basic shelter without tools, tarps or ponchos. The poles can be found lying almost anywhere in the forest and once you have the frame made simply pile forest debris (or even snow) on top. Use an already standing tree as one of your main support beams to provide stability and to save yourself a lot of time and trouble.

See the graphic below for some illustrations of how to construct a very simple forest shelter.

CONSTRUCTING A SHELTER

Pictured above are several examples of how a basic shelter can be fashioned out of almost any available materials.

Shelter in Desert Areas

The desert is generally quite hot during the day and surprisingly cold at night.

Because of limited cloud cover, all ground heat is conducted into the atmosphere when the sun goes down, so any shelter you try to build in a desert environment will need to be adaptable to protect you from both temperature extremes.

Typically, arid regions cannot support large vegetation, which rules out making a big leafy makeshift tent. Any shelter will have be constructed with materials that you are carrying with you, or from natural terrain. Large rocks, crevices and even trenches dug in the sand will provide protection.

To construct a trench shelter, scoop out a trench that is twice as wide as your body and one third longer than your body.

Pile sand along the sides for added cover. Cover over the trench where your body will lay leaving a small area open for ventilation and to use as an entrance/exit. Place an emergency blanket/poncho/vegetation over the trench and weight on both sides with sand enough to hold in place yet. A solar blanket will reflect the sun away during the day and hold the heat from your body in at night.

Before entering your sand shelter, clear the area of scorpions/insects and snakes. Reptiles are cold bloodied and they seek out shade and protection to regulate their body temperature.

Get Off the Ground

If you have the resources, you can construct a sleeping platform that raises your body off the ground. This will help keep insects/reptiles/rodents off of you at night.

Your objective with any shelter, clothing or cover is to contain and regulate your body's temperate. Remember this when considering the use of a sleeping platform. If in a cold climate, ensure you are protected from cold airflow under the sleeping platform by wrapping yourself in a poncho/emergency blanket.

As a bonus, in tropical/hot climates, you can attempt to build your fire so the smoke flows under the bed to help drive away insects. Obviously, take great care to avoid trapping the smoke around you as you could suffocate.

SECTION V.
Makeshift Medical Care

Disaster or not, maintaining a well-stocked first aid kit is essential. As preparation for a potential disaster, make sure to have extended supplies of any prescription medicines that you rely on.

You should always strive to keep a broad, up-to-date selection of medical supplies on hand to provide basic treatment for wounds and to help stabilize the injured until professional medical care can be administered.

It is also useful to know how to use your natural resources to help maintain your health during a crisis situation.

The following methods and techniques are NOT to be considered medical advice and are described for informational purposes ONLY. You should never substitute these methods for professional medical advice or treatment. The methods are only to be attempted when your situation is extremely dire and professional medical treatment is unlikely in the near future.

The Benefits of Cider Vinegar

Many people believe, and certain studies have shown, that consuming apple cider vinegar can help with upset stomach by balancing the Ph level. It's also thought by some, although I remain skeptical, that vinegar (acetic acid) might help to kill E. coli and other harmful bacteria in the stomach.

You can use cider or white vinegar to treat skin rashes and foot fungus by rubbing the vinegar on the rash without diluting. Soak your feet in full strength vinegar to help cure foot fungus (the military describes it as jungle rot). The acetic acid in the vinegar will dilute or render inactive certain plant oils on the skin that can cause rashes. Vinegar can also help sooth insect bites, as well.

It is a good idea to take two tablespoons of cider vinegar, three times daily, if you suspect you have consumed foods or water that may be contaminated. You can also take the recommended dose as a precaution when traveling or in a survival situation. The vinegar will have no ill effects and can only help settle your stomach, regardless of whether you have ingested contaminated water or food.

Using Tobacco

Tobacco is cultivated in many parts of the world. The active component is nicotine, which is found in all parts of the tobacco plant. Some people may experience an allergic reaction to nicotine and nicotine is considered toxic in large doses.

If you suspect or know that you have intestinal parasites caused from drinking contaminated water or eating spoiled food, you can stun or possibly kill the parasites by swallowing a teaspoon (pinch) of smokeless tobacco or by consuming 1.5 to 2 cigarettes. Once stunned or killed by the nicotine, the parasites lose their hold on the intestinal walls and can pass out of the body through the digestive track during a bowel movement. You can repeat the treatment in 24 hours.

Tobacco can also be used as a topical antiseptic/pain treatment for minor wounds, by rubbing the tobacco product over the wound. Tobacco has also been used for centuries as an insect repellent; it is effective when the tobacco leaf is rubbed over the skin.

Purchase a First Aid Kit and Pocket Survival Pak

I always recommend a company called Adventure Medical Kits for anyone looking to purchase a good, quality kit of basic medical supplies to keep on hand.

Check out their website at AdventureMedicalKits.com and consider purchasing a few types of medical kits to cover a variety of situations.

They also sell a really nice pack of rinse-free bathing wipes that allow you to take "waterless showers" on the go. These things are really great; sometimes I will even use them when traveling on long trips with multiple connecting flights. I just duck into an airport restroom.

Being clean makes a big difference in how you feel about yourself, and maintaining good hygiene in a disaster/crisis situation is one of those often-overlooked difference-makers.

Suggested Reading

I strongly advise purchasing a copy of the book "Where There is No Doctor" from an online retailer like Amazon or Barnes & Noble. The reference was originally published in 1992, but a 2010 update adds new and important information.

The book's publisher describes it: "the manual provides practical, easily understood information on how to diagnose, treat, and prevent common diseases. Special attention is focused on mutrition, infection and disease prevention, and diagnostic techniques as primary ways to prevent and treat health problems."

Available for less than $15, you would be wise to purchase a copy today and place it with your emergency medical supplies for safe-keeping.

SECTION VI.
Handling Common Natural Disasters

In our first section, we focused on general preparation steps to be taken in order to protect yourself from a major natural disaster (hurricane, earthquake, etc.) or a more catastrophic calamity like a total economic collapse or the outbreak of an exotic new disease without cure.

Here, we will shift our focus to talk more specifically about coping with a large-scale natural disaster. The biggest difference in how you act, of course, is that there is an expectation that civil society will be restored in relatively short order following a natural disaster.

A major natural disaster can be anything from an earthquake, hurricane or tornado that leaves a suburban neighborhood as a wasteland in its wake. At some point, you stop focusing on the cause and begin to realize that the disaster itself is one thing and surviving in the days after is another.

It takes time to get over the initial shock of any event, even if you had advanced warning.

Panic will set in, which only makes the situation worse. Keep in mind your goal is to sustain life, that is an instinct that is bred into every living creature. Knowledge, preparation, training and practice are the only things that allow people to stifle their panic and continue to carry on in the face of a natural or man-made disaster. We've already gone over some basic stockpiling, now we will talk about putting those tools into use.

In the event of a disaster in which your community's infrastructure is damaged and you do not have an expectation that utilities will be restored for some time, shut the main electrical breaker to the home off and shut off the main gas line. Then, begin to remove perishable items from your refrigerator. Leave the freezer alone for now and avoid opening the door. Refrigerated foods begin to spoil within four to six hours. You do not want the food to spoil in the refrigerator. Cook what you can and consume it the first day.

Place all garbage and spoiled foods as far from the structure as you can. Spoilage will attract insects, rodents and harbor bacteria. Frozen foods in a nonworking freezer can often last up to 48 hours before they become unsafe to eat.

Even though you do not have electrical service, you may be able to draw water from the faucets. Do so as quickly as possible and assume any water from your faucets is contaminated. Breaks in the water line or damage to the water treatment plant can have an effect on the quality of your water. Do not mix this water up with what you have previously stored for an emergency. The water from your tap must be purified to ensure it is safe to drink.

Quick Introduction to Water Collection and Purification

Boiling is always the preferred method to purify water. Therefore, it is important you have a means to start fires and suitable containers to boil water in if you know or suspect any water source is contaminated. Water sources that do require filtering and purification include backyard swimming pools, hot tubs, ponds, lakes, rivers, streams, and open wells. At sea level, a rapid boil for one minute will destroy all harmful contaminates in the water. If you suspect you are well above sea level, rapid boil for three minutes. Air pressure is lower at higher elevations, so water boils at a lower temperature and must therefore boil longer to achieve the same effects as boiling for less time at higher temperatures.

Depending on how prepared you are, and what climate you're located in, it may be wise to begin collecting rainwater in containers as soon as possible. This will be water you have total control over and it should be relatively clean.

Regardless of the source, filter any non-stockpiled water before you begin any type of purification. The ideal filtering medium is activated charcoal. You can also use sand and/or coffee filters if you do not have charcoal. If your source is extremely cloudy, use all three mediums if available, in layers inside of a can or a one-liter bottle with the top cut off. Place several holes in the bottom of your filtering container to allow filtered water to flow out.

Clorox unscented chlorine bleach is the recommended brand to use for water purification. First, filter your water as described above. The ratio to use for treatment is two drops of bleach per one-quart/liter of water. Seal the container, shake well, and allow 30 minutes before drinking. If the water is cloudy after filtering, double the dose to four drops per quart/liter and allow 60 minutes before drinking.

If you're using a Two Percent Liquid Iodine (Tincture of Iodine) to clean your water, go ahead and filter as described above. Then add five drops per one-quart/liter of water, seal the container, shake well and allow 30 minutes before drinking. Same rules apply: if the water is cloudy after filtering, double the dose to 10 drops and allow 60 minutes before drinking. Also, note that it is recommended that you do not drink iodine treated water for more than two weeks at a time.

The First Week Unfolds

As soon as you have verified that everyone in your party is safe, gather all supplies and equipment to conduct a complete inventory. Knowing what resources you have available is step one.

Depending on the type of emergency you're facing, the first 72 hours might also need to be spent inspecting for any structural damage and making any emergency repairs. For insurance purposes, you may not be able to remove downed trees or damaged vehicles until an insurance adjuster has conducted an inspection. Typically, insurance companies expect you to make emergency repairs to the structure to prevent further damage and loss. You should familiarize yourself with your homeowners insurance policy.

A hot meal is in order by the second or third day. Utilize your charcoal grill, propane grill or smoker to provide hot food to yourself and family. Do not cook or operate generators inside of any structure due to the potential for carbon monoxide poisoning.

Monitor your water consumption, because by the fourth and fifth day you and your family members will want to bathe. If your water supply is limited water should only be used for drinking, cooking, oral hygiene and for cleansing of wounds.

If your community or property received water damage, you must be aware of certain dangers associated with pooled and stagnant water. Mosquitoes breed quickly and can carry many nasty diseases. Protect yourself with suitable insect repellent and/or netting.

Deny insects access to your structure by covering any opening with tarps or netting. Keep in mind local wildlife will also be displaced and this includes certain reptiles. Flooding can bring wild animals much closer to human habitation.

By day five and six, you should have established a routine and may have possibly been in contact with local authorities. There may even be local aid stations such as the Red Cross located in your community by this time. The Federal Emergency Management Agency or FEMA may have made contact with your local government. Typically, any aid dispersed is based on immediate needs. Those individuals less prepared than you may very well receive aid first.

Regardless, you are better off if you prepare before the disaster strikes. Why trust your life to the government?

Typical rescue response time is 72 hours. This simply means rescue operations have commenced.

If you are in a remote location, place bright covering materials within view of any highways or logical routes rescue personnel would use, marking your location as best as possible. Typically, emergency personnel will use 911 maps for plotting the locations of homes, so stay near your structure if it is safe to do so.

SECTION VII.
A Final Review

I hope you've found this brief text useful in acquainting you with some basic survival techniques and tactics. Knowing what to do in the event of an emergency will keep you and everyone else calm. Panic is dangerous and counterproductive. You must be organized, take an appropriate leadership role, and make sure everyone has duties assigned to them. Prevent the feeling of helplessness by making sure that everyone stays busy.

In any standard natural disaster situation:

1. Gather and inventory your supplies.
2. Disconnect utilities.
3. Use refrigerated food within 12 hours.
4. Use frozen food within 48 hours.
5. Keep supplies on hand to filter and purify water.
6. Protect your home from insects.
7. Mark your location for rescuers.

8. Document everything for your insurance company.

Your objective is always to provide shelter, water, fire, food, protection and medical care for your family and yourself. Having a reasonable stockpile of select, high-value materials can be the difference between life and death.

Fire is essential for heat, protection, signaling and to purify water and cook food. Knowing a variety of methods for starting a fire can be useful, as you never know what resources will be available to you when disaster strikes.

Remember that tobacco can be used as a topical antiseptic/pain treatment for minor wounds, by rubbing the tobacco product over the wound. Tobacco has also been used for centuries as an insect repellent; it is effective when the tobacco leaf is rubbed over the skin.

In a situation where water is scare, examine the benefits of the water purification techniques we covered when accessing alternative sources of drinking water. Saltwater can be boiled or condensed and the resulting condensation or steam can be consumed, but you must NEVER drink seawater directly.

Above all else, remember that when disaster strikes it will be up to you to take charge, assign duties and maintain calm!

The following are five books that I highly suggest you consider adding to your collection.

1. "Where There Is No Doctor" by the Hesperian Foundation

With millions of copies in print in more than 75 languages, this essential manual provides practical, easily understood information on how to diagnose, treat, and prevent common diseases. Special attention is focused on nutrition, infection and disease prevention, and diagnostic techniques as primary ways to prevent and treat health problems.

2. "Primitive Skills and Crafts" by Linda and Richard Jamison

Anyone eager to master survival skills for outdoor vacations, or simply to find a fun new family activity for a Saturday afternoon, will be educated and inspired by the practical advice presented here by archaeologists, anthropologists, primitive practitioners, craftsmen, and artisans. These experts help modern readers rediscover the skills that have served humanity for millennia: fire-making, camp cooking, basket weaving, pottery making, animal tracking, and much more. You can even learn how to turn seashells into arrowheads or make glue from yucca plants. Plus, there's intriguing information on the benefits of a hunter-gatherer diet.

3. "Mini Farming: Self-Sufficiency on 1/4 Acre" by Brett L. Markham

Even if you have never been a farmer or a gardener, this book covers everything you need to know to get started: buying and saving seeds, starting seedlings, establishing raised beds, soil fertility practices, composting, dealing with pest and disease problems, crop rotation, farm planning, and much more. Because self-sufficiency is the objective, subjects such as raising backyard chickens and home canning are also covered along with numerous methods for keeping costs down and production high.

www.ingramcontent.com/pod-product-compliance
Lightning Source LLC
Chambersburg PA
CBHW050520290526
45786CB00007B/2629